A POET'S
CHOICE

PASCAL R. POLITANO

authorHOUSE®

AuthorHouse™
1663 Liberty Drive
Bloomington, IN 47403
www.authorhouse.com
Phone: 833-262-8899

Published by AuthorHouse 09/29/2022

ISBN: 978-1-7283-2821-8 (sc)
ISBN: 978-1-7283-2822-5 (hc)
ISBN: 978-1-7283-2820-1 (e)

Library of Congress Control Number: 2019914595

Print information available on the last page.

This book is printed on acid-free paper.

Dedicated to Cynthia A. Politano, my "Cordelia," who has never left my side, in both senses.

Contents

A Gathering Storm

The Poet's Corner

What's Love Got To Do With It

The Merchants of Death

Death Be Not Proud

Never Such Innocence Again

Jeux D' Enfants

Bonnie Beasties

En Fin La Paix

A Gathering Storm

A Sharper Seasoning of Truth

And a much shorter one, if you please, than a long book to reveal
All the corners of that very large old canvas called the story of man.
There are times when less is better; when what we so try to conceal
Must be faced and accepted as a fact that we have wished to ban.

We no longer can remain indifferent to what has been our true role.
However much we tell ourselves it's all God's plan and blame fate
For all the ills of the world, and all those evils outside our control.
We must accept the cold reality that any awareness comes too late.

The old men who are most to blame will be spared that final horror.
The rest, who have given those cold-hearted malefactors a reprieve,
Should anyone be left to record our history, will bear the dishonor.
But our abused planet can rest at last, when no one is left to deceive.

So all man's given gifts have availed him nothing, it is sad to say.
But then, sadly also, you cannot make a good pot out of poor clay.*

---

* Or as the Germans would have it, more eloquently, *Aus so krummem Holz, als woraus der Mensch gemacht ist, kann nichts ganz Gerades gezimmert warden*— Out of the crooked timber of humanity no straight thing can ever be made.

The Lamps Are Going Out

That was Grey of Fallodon's ominously grim prognostication,
As he watched the lamplighters on the eve of the Great War.
I predict matters more dire, not in Europe, but in this nation.

The dismal blackouts of that next war, a greater conflagration,
Will be as nothing when they are compared to what is in store.
When our Grid goes down, there will be total, utter desolation.

The cheery song "When the Lights Go on Again" (a re-creation)
Will have lost its meaning, like a key that fits no locked door.
Look where you will, you will find no electro-communication.

No lights, no TV, no phones—smart, or by any other classification.
No power tools, no air conditioning or video games, what's more.
And cadmium-ion batteries don't last forever (another damnation!)

We've been caught in our own worldwide web of electrification,
Like Byron's eagle no longer through rolling clouds could soar,
Whose own feather winged the dart that brought his annihilation.

Electricity, one of the oldest sources of power of man's creation,
And the *sine qua non* for the myriad newest devices we so adore,
Taken for granted for so long, like an old, dependable relation,
Will die, suddenly, and take with him all our great expectations.

Come Back, Little Phoebus?

"Little" because, comparatively, Phoebus is;
but merely in a relative, comparative sense.
Relative as in "cut him out in *little* stars ...."
There are stars out there which make ours
look insignificant, miniscule by comparison.
But, he *is ours*, and "little" is not demeaning
but amiable, like Li'l Doggie, or Little Darlin'.

Climate change? Our willful gas keeps heat in,
but fortunately it also keeps some rays out,
or we'd all fry, so somehow we're grateful.
Come back? Are we begging spring to return,
tired of all the snow, sleet, and chilling wind?
But will we miss those much maligned effects
when Phoebus triumphs, winter is no more, and
blazing summer becomes an unendurable hell?

Or are we just pining for those happier days,
when we were young; saw things differently?
Those golden days of youth (*gaudeamus igitur*),
when sunrise and sunset had more meaning,
something more than dawning or end of day?

Do we fear that Phoebus will go, of an evening,
and not return till the next blessed morning?
Fear not; for The sun also ariseth, we are told,
and though the Good Book reassures us that
it shall not smite thee by day, we may someday

wish to hold back that dawn which will come up:
a horror we'll have learned to dread—like thunder,
an inferno—not merely "outer China 'crost the Bay!"

That "Lucky Ol' Sun" Frankie Lane sang about
may continue to "roll aroun' heaven all day,"
and we may continue to thank God for that,
until he becomes *nemesis*: our mortal enemy.
Then Phoebus no longer will be seen as "little,"
by any standard or comparison, but will become
the ogre we saw as children, come to devour us.

Political *What?*

More to the point: craven dishonesty.
What has politics got to do with it?
Well, ask Donna Shalala, or the late
Leo Buscaglia, with his hugging cult.
And euphemism is in the catbird seat.
(Not *blind,* merely "visually impaired.")
Did all this fatuous exaltation begin
when a janitor emerged as a custodian
and a garbage man a sanitary engineer?

Whatever happened to "discriminating"?
"discerning"? "selective"? or even "choosy"?
as well as afflicted, crippled, dim-witted,

ugly,* ignorant, retarded, and a plethora of
other undeniably descriptive adjectives?
You can't say you're "right" about anything
because that would imply that somewhere,
someone out there is *wrong*—anathema!

And we butcher the only language we have,
so as to satisfy feminism's dusky divinities—
("Each [one] must do *their* [his or her] duty.")
"I'm okay, you're okay"—*sancte* self-esteem!

In its legitimate sense, *political correctness*
merely should insist upon honesty, justice,
and a *genuine* regard for *all* the nation's polity.

So go on and hug all those wretches you see,
but just keep your silly, sticky hands off me.

Western Civ

Poli sci, English lit, and social psych,
backpacks, blue jeans, and a bike,
math, phys ed, and a water bed,
and a Walkman while we hike;
trig, Coke, Reeboks, and the like,

---

* As in Winston Churchill's alleged response to the horse-faced woman who complained
that he was drunk: "Perhaps I am drunk; but tomorrow I'll be sober, Madam, and you'll
still be ugly."

lines, and "lines," and lines of type;
student loans and tow-away zones,
Soweto shacks and other hype...

Tons of tomes and technics tedious,
scribblers various, works hilarious;
too much too soon—who calls the tune,
the *maitre* or the class buffoon?
Both look the same, each bears the shame;
in this Yard of browsing cattle
the ancient muse, afraid to fly,
becomes a common chattel.

Do not unscrew a fountain pen
and put it to the page, my friend,
that ballpoint in your mouth will do;
or just tape it, end to end.
If Mrs. Eliot could put on her glasses
she'd see how these asses
have brought forth a pox
from her son's magic box
reaching back to Mount Parnassus.

T.S., old boy, your talent was real, but
they took your ideal as a license to steal;
their words, like most whores',
don't inspire, they bore, like the "art"
of an "artist" who throws paint from a loft to a floor.
Our language which once was in such strong solution,
like its Favonian forebear now spreads everywhere

In progressive diminution.
No Latin or Greek, and our French is weak—
what's wrong with you tourists, *why* can't you speak?
We now fly to Byzantium; there's no time to spare
To study its history or language or care
what to *feel*, not just see, once we are there.
Clear is the goal: Go for the gold!
Platonic reflection's an art grown cold;
success is not measured in terms of the old.

But other magic boxes, in and out of school,
tell us how to speak and act
and so have come to rule
our thoughts, our dreams, the way we look—
how can we "learn" if we can't read a book?
So now we're taught to smile as we recite:
"My son was shot to death last night,"
using gestures learned the day before
while watching "Guiding Light."

Video games and using first names
won't bring the world together;
we can't hide from the nuclear age,
national rage, and terror. Don't you see?
All the world's a cage, not a stage
where a tin-voiced parvenu
can sing about his view.
(Can they be wrong, with approval so strong?
(Surely they'd panic without devices galvanic?)

Western civ and the way we live,
with lots of noise and the girls and boys
who would like to live for ever,
cocaine trips, computer chips, and
satellites predicting the weather....
What will it take before we can break
this corrosive concatenation?
Perhaps we can start by dropping the "civ,"
and moving on with civilization.

Ex Libris

Those who called radio the theater of the mind,
when they think of books will also find
that they, the books, have better pictures
than TV or movies, those graphic mixtures
of sex and violence served up on the half-shell,
whose endless production seems never to sate
the cravings of our illiterate modern masses—
indifferent, unschooled in the gems of Parnassus,
oblivious to the beauty of the written word,
they enjoy nothing unless it's seen or heard,
but spoken not by their own inner voices;
they let some dumb arbiter make their choices.

Sex and violence need no interpretation,
and special effects have little relation,
offer no explanation for the human condition.
The only consolation seems to lie in perdition.

Do you prefer a child raised on random curses
to one who begins with *A Garden of Verses*?
And that lissome lass who lived next door
now proudly depicts the rough-shod whore
who matches, word for word, the ill-bred bore
whose tasteless crippled speech is larded over
with speech once reserved for barrack room play,
which are merely tired commonplaces today.

A word people use today I need hardly mention
has become so trite, a casual convention,
that it (and its derivatives), once so pungent,
has become merely a conversational unguent.
One senses that even as he removes her clothing
he treats her nonetheless with a fine loathing.
Can the intellect still crave acute interpretation,
or is it doomed to this diet of pure devastation?

Some books contain these same bromides, you say.
Oh, yes, I say, indeed they do flaunt the same clichés;
but they must compete, you see, to do their best,
to end as films; then they'll be just like all the rest.
But those are books of modern stamp,
whose authors burn no midnight lamp,
but mainly speak those words of sex and rage.
then hasten them on "camera ready" to the page.

But there still are books—written long before
formulaic bullet strikes and their attendant gore,
or chases ending in such pyrolytic auto smashes

one wonders if there's an oil drum in the ashes—
numberless old books, many covered in dust
since they lack that essential violence and lust.
with "special effects" of their own—like simile,
symbolism, imagery, and metaphor, metonymy—
effects which the writer must so carefully place,
that their meaning does not explode in one's face,
which perhaps makes us not a little less but more
than human rubbish, mere sweepings off the floor.

Cosmology 201[*]

The mystery of those terrifying galactic black holes
has been solved: We're in one of our own making.
But if we're not, perhaps those mad scientists
on the Swiss-French frontier can create one
with their seventeen-mile accelerator,
which, however small, might destroy
our weary Earth and so spare us
the agony of self-destruction,
the incremental devastation
caused by global warming
combined with the mad
financial avarice of
Wall Street and
otherwhere.
Finis?

•

---

[*] The title was chosen simply because a poem entitled "Cosmology 101" exists elsewhere
in my published poetry.

Hearts and Minds

A Guerrilla is a fish which must swim in a friendly sea.
Thus Chairman Mao's wise and irrefutable pronouncement.
We knew this almost seventy years ago. From the 1950s
we've been referring to that maxim, less poetically perhaps,
as "Winning the hearts and minds of the people," a phrase
made popular by those pseudo intellectual practitioners of
Psywar, then Psyop, on "Smoke Bomb Hill," at Ft. Bragg.

Oh yes; there was plenty of historical evidence attesting
to the wisdom of that policy: Special Forces soldiers were
required to speak at least one foreign language, and engaged
in intensive Area Studies on the culture, politics, economics,
geography, and so on, of countries of interest. And it was not
unusual, at that Center at Ft. Bragg, to see a "Green Beret"
in the library there reading a newspaper or other periodical
written in a foreign language. Oh, some of us knew what we
should be doing, all right: digging that new village well, and
providing basic medical care, and building roads, improving
our language skills; not providing TV sets where there was
no electricity, to broadcast not seeds, but our own propaganda.

But then one President knew his Special Counsel had a sign
hung above his head for all the world to see and which read:
"Get 'em By The Balls And Their Hearts And Minds Will Follow."
Relentlessly, we have pursued that infantile, wrongheaded,
bully-boy policy throughout the world, again, again, and again,
striking out left, right, and center at anyone who disagrees.
Now, like a black frost, we are blighting the Garden of Allah.

What can anyone do about this blind travesty and injustice?
Occasionally, in Antigua, as I stand thigh-deep in its tranquil
translucent, turquoise waters, I watch the barracudas glide by.
Those benign barracudas have stared at me with curiosity,
even with a degree of interest, but not once with hostility.

Non c' è Niente da Fare

Not to be outdone by the Germans (The Munich-Hamburg Express
will be one minute late), the Italian announcer intones:
The Messina-Rome Express will be one hundred eighty minutes late (!).
The well-dressed man turns to his wife and with a shrug sighs:
Non c' è Niente da Fare....
And the station restaurant is closed and locked
for *riposo* (as in siesta) over the next three hours.

Our train has left the station, more or less on time,
for an uncertain, an unknown destination,
and I'm on it, and you're on it—we're *all* on it,
bound for only God really knows where....

Now we have crossed the last lofty trestle,
with its limitless view of distant horizons,
over a frighteningly fathomless chasm below;
left far behind those last lovely Elysian fields,
strewn with brilliant blossoms where once
we saw our more docile fellow creatures
grazing contentedly on long, lush, green grass.

Now we are going through the last, long, dim tunnel,
a tunnel which will have no light at its end,
however desperately we may seek to see its glow.
Wherever our destination it won't be like anything
we've ever experienced; surely, it will be interesting,
if only in the sense of an ancient Chinese curse.

You see, we have already passed the tipping point:
self-inflicted climate change; economics; genocide;
it is too late, much too late, and we cannot stop.
We *might* have done it....Now nothing *can* be done.
Non c' è Niente da Fare—there is nothing to be done.

La Commedia è Finita[*]

It's finished, over;
if our ship of state doesn't sink
it'll be just another burnt-out case,
as we once described survivors of leprosy.
The financial sector, Uncle Milty's[†] free market,
along with government complicity, has done us in.
Eccola; la gente paga,[‡] and our great grandchildren, or
even *their* children won't be able to pay the debt.
The Grade "B" (at best) Actor-President's policy of
"If we give to the rich the poor shall thrive."
was just moonshine; smoke and mirrors.
So have the poor in their thriving
obliterated the middle class?
But why then are the poor,
now with millions
dispossessed,
poorer?

Why are they being driven out of their homes?
Why should they be sleeping in their cars?
(if those have not been repossessed also).
Why are they begging in those food pantries?

---

[*] The comedy is ended.

[†] President Reagan's favorite economist, Milton Friedman, of the University of Chicago.

[‡] So there it is; the people pay.

But are matters truly so bad?
Well, when we have hit rock bottom
there won't be any inflation to worry us,
that's what a *Depression* is all about (think 1930s),
so we'll be able to buy almost everything for just a nickel:
a hot dog, a beer, a candy bar, a phone call, or a subway ride;
But this time those CEOs won't be selling those five-cent apples;
(*q.v.* Bing Crosby's evocative "Brother, Can You Spare a Dime?");
riding golden parachutes, they'll be landing in the Hamptons
or on estates in those breezy-balmy off-shore islands.
So this time you won't have to worry about
walking under tall Manhattan buildings;
there won't be any jumping there,
to avoid the poverty, or an
indictment, or, too rarely,
the shame.

A shambles, and truly a nation of sheep, who remain docile
as they are led to the slaughter....But look on the bright side:
Bacon & Eggs-25¢! Bowl of Chili-25¢! Franks and Beans-25¢!
(if you manage to find a quarter in your pocket or your purse).

The Poet's Corner

That Ceaseless Succession

How many, many times do those idle thoughts come?
They come in ceaselessly; they override one another,
Like waves coming ashore from a vast sea of memories.
They recede into endless others that come hastening in
To beat relentlessly upon a tired shore, wearing it away,
Imperceptibly for a time, but at last revealing their vast
Inroads into what once was solid earth. On they come,
Then go, leaving at times flotsam and jetsam of the past,
Leaving nothing of value, except to those idle combers
Of shorelines who, too infrequently, find something that
They, gentle scavengers, think might be worth keeping.

That Ineffable Silence

A crowded room; twenty or thirty people;
men, women, young, old, dressed anyhow—
to the nines, or like slovenly clowns—
(one wonders how clean their linen is,
if they're wearing any). Women no longer
use handkerchiefs; they wipe away tears
of joy, or grief, affectedly, with their hands.
One looks, and like Webster sees the skull

beneath the skin, and worse...and one knows
that however fair and smooth that skin, alas,
universal stench and corruption lie within.

Noise; loud, raucous at times, and the clink
and clash of china, crystal, silver, and ice;
the usual belch, or sneeze, or cough (or worse)
(Kurt Masur went home to Leipzig, disgusted
by the persistent coughing of his audiences).
Here are even guffaws and shrieks of laughter....

And then, abruptly, a hush, absolute silence.
Suddenly, that mystical, magical moment....
Not a sound, not a clink, a voice, a whisper.
A silent assemblage, a momentary *tableau,*
all suddenly are struck dumb in an instant....

It happens, and is undeniable by anyone who
has lived long enough to have experienced it;
but the phenomenon itself is inexplicable.
Still, one or more of those arrogant scientists
(but not Einstein, humble enough to admit God)
who are fanatically driven to have an answer
for *everything,* would, somehow, "explain it,"
using calculus (algorithm is an "in" term now).

Someone, a skeptic, once told me it was God;
God demanding our attention for that moment;
then of course he added with a cynical smile:
but now we're listening, why won't He speak?

("Attention all hands! The Captain has the word!"
Silence. A voice: "Why don't he share it wid us?")
I told him that silence doesn't imply listening.
I cannot compare myself with Einstein, but
when next I'm struck dumb, I'm going to listen.

Painting the Lily

To gild refined gold, to paint the lily,
To throw a perfume on the violet,
To smooth the ice, or add another hue
Unto the rainbow, or with taper-light
To seek the beauteous light of heaven to garnish,
Is wasteful and ridiculous excess.

Oh yes; how I *wish* I'd written that;
could have written that!
Of course, that was the Sweet Swan of Avon
(or Marlowe, some would argue);
yet, why seek to write something better,
when that says it so utterly?

Some things cannot be improved upon, full stop.
Keep what's tried and true as it is,
and concentrate on what still is possible,
what truly is new, and perhaps, *better.*
No, don't bring back the Tug of War to the Olympics;
some things will fall under their own weight;
and I won't speak of quantum advances in technology,

except to say that I think Prince Charles was
right when he asked: "Do we command technology,
or have we become its slaves?"
But what of art, all art: what was, now is, produced?
Some black and white photos *abhor* color!

Don't tell a Neapolitan chef *Broccoli Lasagna* is *lasagna*;
don't ask a German bartender for *peppermint* Schnapps,
or his Russian counterpart for *blueberry* vodka;
don't tell Lou Gehrig about the benefits of HGH;
don't tell Manet that throwing darts at balloons filled
with varicolored paints and pinned to a wall is art;
don't tell Tennyson that our American Poet Laureate
(or any *North* American in recent history) writes poetry,
or P.G. Wodehouse that he had to peddle dirt to be popular;
don't tell the manager of that exquisite Paris Opera House
that that warehouse in Baltimore also is an opera house;
don't tell Beethoven that the Nashville notation system
is written music; and in the same vein, don't tell Segovia
that Willy Nelson or Johnny Cash play(ed) the guitar;
("Fresh ink"? Yes all music once *was* new; but old or new,
there are only two kinds of music—good, and bad.)

I'd better stop here or *I'll* be guilty of painting the lily,
when all I'm trying to do is point to it.
But remember: *Plus* ça *change, plus c'est la même chose,*
which in many cases is not a bad thing.

The Tentative Transport of Joy

Are joy and sorrow truly one?
Do our joys in age diminish?
Is pain undone when life is done?
Or are our joys pilfered at the finish?

Can a bitter joy hear the sound of wings?
Is our feast of bliss but a dish of pain?
Are friendship, love, and other things
Purged away and only regret remain?

Do past joys perish in the deluge of our grief?
At the end do we feel neither pain nor pleasure?
But if joy comes again, quietly, subtly, like a thief,
Cannot a frozen heart wake and grasp the treasure?

The weariness of hope deferred renders joy a knave.
The spirit, long dead, merely watches from its grave.

Un Ballo in Maschera

They all were masked "in masks outrageous and austere"
except, oh, perhaps just a few who'd refused the mask.
The costumiers had had a most difficult time; for the theme
was not historical, musical, literary, societal, or other of
the usual motifs of such a lavish mid-winter's event,
but the personification of human traits, and the more the better.
and to whom, not surprisingly, no one paid much attention.

There, one saw the artful mask of Guile; there the crafty face of
Avarice, and there, near the flushed puffed up smile of Pride, the
spiteful countenance of Envy. Sloth danced with Greed, and Lust
was everywhere (perhaps the easiest mask of all). Grief sat alone,
while the vincible visage of Fear quailed before Rage, and
here and there one saw the quiet mask of Indifference; and suddenly,
the unadorned faces of those unmasked seemed strikingly "new."

They danced all night long (or short, if you think of it that way),
and with the dawn they went their separate ways, and then
most, the masked ones mainly, went to sleep, but slept
uneasily, were restless in the thin light of day; and some,
mostly unmasked, didn't sleep, but went on with their lives,
as if that night of frenetic revelry had never been....
Perhaps Congreve was right: to go naked is the best disguise.

Al-Quahirah

Galabiyas sway as men with dusty hands and feet
move dusty rocks at break of day,
and women in black don't smile as shadows shrink;
they cannot eat or drink for one day more as
they work beside the Nile.
A wizened desert-man with an old Enfield rifle
who stands guard unbidden while his camel's
not ridden in the shadow of the tombs, and radios begin
to boom the husky songs of Um Kulthum,
as the sun comes up over Cairo.

Stale cigarettes and attar of roses,
sticky sweets and syrupy soda,
the sweat and smell of the *souk*;
a fez for two pounds, and roses with
thorns so big they can wound (for two pounds).
Brass-plated coffee pots, flimsy and gaudy,
cheap imitations of their earlier cousins;
tourists, uncaring, buy them in dozens.
The dim, cool recess at the back of the flat,
where the rubbish boy stands mid myriad cats,
hungry and silent, wide-eyed, mysterious;
both he and these cats, eerily serious,
peer through the gloom like Pharaonic idols,
while the sun shines down on Cairo.

A beautiful building in Garden City has
a hole in its side so a Carrier can provide
that rare air in which foreigners abide,
while the news in the papers stuffed round the
breach speak of hope, and a new agricultural goal.
Trees with brown leaves line the *Corniche,*
while cars in their hundreds deny any speech.
The once-lovely Gezira on its isle in the Nile...
but why should *Auslanders* be arbiters of style?
Shepheards' Phoenix dwarfed by the Meridien,
as well as the Hilton and Sheraton (but when
Egyptians rebel they burn the best Western hotels),
as the sun blazes down on Cairo.

A voice from a window sings a song of regret,
a trans-river *felluca* for two cigarettes...
The boatman works his sail and frowns, but
I know he is grateful when I do not smoke
because he cannot till the sun goes down.
The quick in Dead City live on and in the tombs,
since the Silent Majority has the authority
to provide the living with rent-free rooms.
In this teeming city, where need grinds one's heart to dust;
there is little hope, small pity, and even less that's just.
Still, there is a stately, mannered dignity among
these millions in pain, and a strange paradox of
generosity that I really cannot explain.
But soon these children of the Nile will have
Relief—well, if only for a little while...
as the sun sinks low in Cairo.

Ramadan has passed; it's time for celebration.
They'll kill a goat and break their fast and
though our Gods have different names and I
am from a distant, different place, they tell me
I can join them all the same in this feast
which they call *Bairam*. (But can this fellah have a Stella?
—better that I go.) Their offer is kind, but will they mind
if I pretend that I cannot stay? For they are not of me
nor am I of them, and though I've had a pleasant day
it is better that I go, to a wine shop I know—
while they celebrate their *Bairam*—where for
only two pounds there are to be found
Cleopatra, Nefertiti, and Omar Kayam,
as the sun falls away from Cairo.

White Shadows
(Standing The White Man's Burden on its Head)

Surely, a snow-white wedding gown is no guarantor of chastity
    or purity,
and a charging red-eyed white rhino* will kill you just as surely
    as will its black brother.
Those awed and terror-stricken Alpine villagers find no beauty
    in the approaching avalanche,
and snow blindness and "white-outs" in frosty northern climes
    inspire no enthusiasm.

But the white shadow, due to its very nature—unseen, invisible—
    is deadlier than its black brothers,
and somehow works a curious phenomenon: *black shadows vanish*
    in the wake of their white cousins!
Therein lies the hazard: when it passes, its work has been done;
    its path has been cleared,
and never, never will those teeming places which it has crossed
    be the same again.

Yes, those other white hazards become truly pale by comparison
    to the white shadow—
for after The Great White Shadow had passed over those darker parts
    of the planet
avalanches, blizzards, blindness, charging rhinos, whorish brides,
    all would have been welcomed in its stead.
One could ask: "Who knows what evil lurks in the hearts of men? and be
    answered, "The Shadow knows...."

---

* Now extinct, thanks to those avaricious ivory poachers and their calloused Asian consumers.

An Insurmountable Bitterness

There's no gainsaying it; it has been here for some four hundred years.
It has haunted us for almost half that time; but no, not enough of us.
(Though some have felt a bit of what has brought those others to tears.)

But those of us who have not and who's unreceptive and uncaring ears
Are deaf to the unendurable frustration that has been suffered silently
By those who have been living in the dark shadows of their white peers.

"Fats" Waller's singing of "Black and Blue" said it, evoking no cheers:
And Toni Morrison, then a girl, prayed that she might have blue eyes;
And her later fame would, in the minds of some, be greeted with sneers.

To say "Black is beautiful" was seen as only a feeble attempt to steer
The ship of fair play closer to some just parity with those whose ship
Already had berthed safely at *their* birth, so *they* had nothing to fear.

The words sound silly to one who cleaves to certain unexpressed fears
That somehow those others might rise up and challenge their own ranks
Of supremacy, though which now, social correctness has made less clear.

What will continue is that whole-souled, searing ache that will appear
When to poor wretches like Michael Jackson mirrors must ever reveal
That however much his people strive for elevation through their careers,
They never can, never will, until we all are coated with the same veneer.

Snow Diamonds

really aren't diamonds at all (as one sees
when one gets too close, or even changes position,
on a crackling-clear, sunny, but bitterly cold day).
You can't gather them, harvest them, even touch them;
and they vanish if you move your vantage point
even by just a millimeter. And you can't sell them,
you can't wear them; but you can see them, enjoy them,
from a distance, until conditions change; and
they *are* as beautiful (blue, or yellow, or blue-yellow,
glinting brilliantly where they lie, a little like certain
tiny Christmas tree lights that wink on and off) as those
ancient other superheated lumps of carbon men and
women literally die for. —But how can I describe these
elusive beautiful brilliants? —It's something like
looking at the stars on a clear night: beautiful, and yet
unapproachable (and if we could get there, to the stars—
just think a moment—there'd be no more beauty in them,
we'd find only a superheated, gaseous horror....)

You can see, and touch, and hold the tiny diamond earrings
some women like to wear, sparkling and pretty, even if
they're man-made, synthetic, or fake, or whatever you may
wish to call them. —Ah, but these snow diamonds though!
They're absolutely beautiful, and they're *real*—we can
see them, sprinkled here and there, oh, any old way, there
on their frosty ermine-carpeted field—elusive, ephemeral,

untouchable, unusable, even unapproachable.... And therein
lies their mystique: they are only to be admired, enjoyed,
perhaps even loved (if that is not too strong a word for you).
These little brilliants are not to be worn, or even touched;
and they certainly are not to be bought, or sold, or hoarded—

Just treasured.

The Dark Woods

The people up here, North Country folk,
call them only that: "the dark woods";
it seems they have no other name, of a
person, place, tribe. Haunted, some joke.
Amusing to some it may be—but a joke?
I don't think so when I hear the children
or the older people whispering about it.
But I'm too new to question them or poke
into such local matters; I'm out to please
these new neighbors, and so I just smile
and start to say that in my travels of this
weary world I've heard some tales of trees...
Not haunted! they're quick to make it clear,
but still, there is something you see when
you look into their eyes; as they look away
you see—something, that could be fear.
Some say it's just the wind from Tug hill,
but then how can *they,* on those brittle
winter's nights, how can they call to you
on those cold dead nights when all is still?

You must be close by them, must get near,
for they do not call loudly; you just listen
for their soft susurrations, must get closer
to the edge of that forest, so you can hear.
But, say some, Do not go among those trees!
however sweet and strong their siren song;
though they offer refuge, keep to the road
however keen comes that frigid breeze.

I have no little horse, just this little jeep, but
Oh, those Frosty woods, so lovely, dark and deep!
Ah, yes….But I have no more promises to keep,
and such a brief, short way to go before I sleep.*

A Pearl in My Foul Oyster

To see the person across the room
who has just ingested a bad oyster
can put you off your own provender.
To swallow one yourself is worse.†

Oh, but to find in *your* foul oyster
a treasure, *a pearl without price!*
Well, devour that bivalve if you can,
but do spare the opalescent droplet.

---

* Evocative of Robert Frost's, perhaps too obviously, "Stopping by Woods on a Snowy Evening."

† "He was a bold man that first eat an oyster," said Dean Swift.

Yes, that pearl—divine concretion!
Rich honesty dwells like a miser
in a poor house, as your foul oyster,
or so the Swan of Avon has told us.

Indeed, I ate the offensive bivalve;
(it's taken forever to lose the taste).
I didn't eat the pearl; no, I saved it,
and I will not cast it before swine.

The Demands of Honors

> For unto whomsoever
> much is given, of him
> shall be much required
> St. Luke 12:48

Congratulations! Well done! another degree!
Put those laurels up on your wall, if you will;
you have every right to, as we all would agree.

And from time to time you'll look up and see
the stately phrases that attest to your skill
and feel a just pride in that hard-won Ph.D.

You may decide on a rest now that you are free
(except for the small matter of all those bills);
all creatures must relax, even the busiest bee.

No lectures, books, essays; not one more fee.
No late nights (so groggy you resort to a pill).
Yes, that's all done with; do go have a spree!

But do reflect, now you've climbed that tree,
there's more to do, an even greater task to fill.
With success must come its attendant duty.

Don't glory in those honors as you look with glee
or as you point them out to friends (worse still).
Though your sails seem full, you're still at sea.

Congratulations! Well done! Another degree!
But put that degree to work; be what you can be.

Think Small

The whole world is suffering—can I do anything about that?
I would if I could, but I can't. Probably no one can, or will....
But Rosie is at the vet's, the best one I could find,
who will do all that's needed to ensure that she gets well.

So, in a way, I'm thinking small, or thinking big in a small way;
yes, perhaps I'm thinking as big as my limited power permits.

Anyway, I'm doing what I can. I do not know, nor can I help
all the wretched of the earth, but I know and can help Rosie.

Though limited, I can help Rosie, with more than hopes or wishes;
I don't have to pine, pity, or pray as for all those beyond my means.

What could or should be done (but probably never will be done),
by those mightier or abler than I is, like the stars, beyond my grasp.

So yes; I will continue to think small (after all, that is so very human),
and doing so will accomplish more than all those with greater power.

What's Love Got To Do With It

The Tragedy of Love

What? He died young, in the war, you say?
What's that? She died suddenly of some illness?
What is that you say? His parents got in their way?
What was that? Hers sent her abroad in distress?

O tragedy of tragedies! Oh, sorrow of sorrows!
To long for the one you love with all your heart,
The one you could not wait to see tomorrow,
To bear the anguish, the heartache it was to part!

To suffer those sorrows when one's yearning,
At its height, lends a splendor to all life's sorrows;
A flame glowing gemlike, still brightly burning,
Longs for those reunions on the snail-paced morrows.

But no, in those sad partings lies not the true anguish:
Behold, there is a poisoned dart in Cupid's quiver,
A less tangible force that makes love languish;
A waste that towards its mouth pollutes love's river.

No, the subtle, ruthless fiend who slowly blights
The bloom of love and sunders early bliss—
As one or other ceases caring, loses the light—
Is *indifference*, that spectral, patient witness.*

Croce Felice

A double anguish (the agony comes like a blow)
For someone you cannot *not* love, for that Other.
Love kills; if you never loved how can you know?

You're swept up, carried along in the flow
Of the agony and distress of sister or brother,
as implacably she, or he, is laid down below.

Still worse, on a leaden day, there, in the snow.
you watch as they lower your father or mother
deep, deep, with creak of the ropes—slow, slow.

(You stood there rooted, with a toddler in tow—
while a doctor neared, anxious nurse hovered—
close by the child whose tears had begun to flow.)

---

* Or as Juan Montalvo (1832-1889) put it: "There is nothing harder than the softness of indifference."

For God's sake, hurry it up! You there—throw
that black earth in there; hurry, hurry, and cover
that grey box; fill in that raw hole, so I can go!

But why punish *me* through them? Is this but a show?
The worse punishment through which I may discover
Your *Croce Felice,* that cheerful cross to set me aglow?
I—whose blithe and happy heart already *was* all aglow?

Loosely Labeled Love

Some words today, like the flight of a dove,
Leave no trace in their wake and often mislead;
No exception is today's meaning of "love."

Labels written or spoken (as mentioned above),
May describe the deed, but not the *need*;
Why this loose meaning we've attached to Love?

The word should be treasured, from a child's "wuv"
Through all the expressions we hear and read—
I truly mourn for the one we have lost for "Love."

"Yes, I was with him," she says. "We 'made love'."
While what she means is they thrashed in the weeds.
Keep it clear when it's simply sex you're speaking of!

Call it sex, lust, or intercourse, or worse Guv,

But, "What's Love got to do with it?" I plead.

Why this base meaning we've attached to Love?

Quit this loose meaning we've attached to Love!"

A Disenchanting Dichotomy

Lies in the way we see ourselves, desire and want ourselves to be;
not accepting how we truly are. We set our own standards much like
a child "hiding" its own Easter eggs—despite all the evidence at hand
that we are disgusting, we gloat. Mere arrogance and blind conceit?
We make much of eating (not dining); to some Epicureans it is an art form,
which must ignore what follows: the digestive process, with its
inevitable and noisome conclusion. While we seek physical perfection
we ignore the inescapable realities innately linked to our physicality.

Fleet Street Ditch had its purpose. The Glaswegian chamber maid who
shouted "Guardy loo!" (*Garde l'eau*) as she hurled the morning's slops
from a window to the street below wasn't extolling her lady's charms.
But would she have described her, clinically, as a tube within a tube,
three-quarters full of excrement, as would the gastroenterologist?

I suppose we glorify the human body because it's the only one we're given,
although scientists will admit openly it's the filthiest thing on the earth.

What Do They Want?

Her phone number becomes unique;
when you hear those very numbers
they are set apart from all others
(even the six million of the Holocaust).
Think of "On the Street Where You Live";
the street becomes a sacred place,
there's no other like it, anywhere, but
only because "she" lives in its precincts.
In *Oklahoma*, it's her rose and her glove.

But also in *My Fair Lady*, it's—"Show Me!"
And in that oldie, "If it happens, let it
happen; I don't care…" (let *what* happen?)
What does all this fervor mean? Is she to
be idolized, adored from a distance, or
taken brusquely and galloped strenuously?

What does she want? Freud couldn't say.
She may enjoy the former niceties awhile,
but at bottom (if you will permit the word),
she grows increasingly to want the latter.
Women always were, are, and always will
be more sensible than men care to admit.

The Second Honeymoon

"Listen, darlin'; before we shuffle off
this mortal coil, let's shuffle off to Buffalo again.
We can go back to that old hotel
where we stayed in Niagara Falls back in '87."
"That's great! Oh George, let's do it! It'll be heaven.

"Is that your packing list? Let me see it, honey!"—
"We'll need support hose, Preparation-H, corn plasters—"
"What're *those, Viv ?*" "Sofkins Flushable Cleansing Wipes.
I get the generic ones from Rite-Aid; they're a lot cheaper,
you know, and they've got aloes!"

"I bet the hotel's even got blue movies now, on TV!"
"Hell, who needs 'em? You got me!"
"Okay! If you've got the Viagra, then let's hit Niagara!"

She wears stretch pants to hide the varicose veins
and cellulite; his blue jeans hide the two-foot,
triple-bypass scar which disfigures his left leg.

In their honeymoon suite of yore she giggles as,
naked, he goes to shut the window.
"The first time we were here you looked like a Greek god.
Now you look like a goddam Greek!"
"Very funny, Vivian! But that doesn't hurt me—
What's troublesome is your lack of P.C."

So uncaring and blissfully they go along, none the wiser,
trusting not so much in God but in the science of Pfizer.

The Embrace

When one is young and still impressionable
even the smell of wool, even of cheap wool,
nay, even of cheap, wet wool (as when her
winter coat had gotten drenched in a rainfall),
is memorable, and cherishable.
And apropos of that example,
smell sometimes is the most lasting,
the most vivid of all our sensory memories.

A chill winter's night, the front porch,
warm clothing, her cold cheek but
inner warmth, the scent of her perfume
(later you would buy her some you couldn't afford),
the heady smell of her silken, newly-washed hair,
its highlights of auburn tints….

A weakness in the knees at that first-ever-tasted
real kiss, a stronger embrace, and another,
longer kiss, the aftertaste of lip rouge,
all the senses heightened—everything—
the gleam of a wet tooth, of an earring,
her delicate smooth flesh, the green flash
of silk scarf which smelled slightly of her,
even her shoes—so flimsy, stylish, small—
everything, remembered as if it just happened.
Was it Shaw who said you have to die to know love…?

Then, when I tried to explain, to capture all this,
that philistine medical student—who critically,
coldly described a woman as a tube within a tube,
usually about three-quarters full of excrement.
As much as I hated to hear it, then, at that time;
now, when I see a woman, even a beautiful woman,
it seems to be all I that can think of....
I've also begun to see them as skeletons,
covered with more or less attractive flesh.
Perhaps this is one of the benefits of dying young—
it's a way away from cynicism; one can remember,
one still can remember...and keep one's ideals....

Rusalka's Quest[*]

Well, here was this pretty little water sprite,
living what I would call an idyllic little life
in a quaint little pond in the Bohemian woods,
the outlook of a pleasant eternity before her.

But despite all this she wants to be human
so that she can love the invariable prince.
Her wish granted, she takes a human form,
thereby incurring all those human afflictions.

---

[*] With a nod to Antonin Dvôrák.

Breast and cervical cancer; to say nothing
of diarrhea, flatulence, menstrual problems,
dermal defects, hair loss, dental problems:
all the myriad maladies which women face.

Freud asked: What do women want? I ask:
What would they bear just to "get a little"?
Was Rusalka's pleasure equal to her woes?
Or the prince's, with this spritely spectre?

Rosalie

The dawn lights up my bed a little;
I wake to another, shorter day.
The old ache won't let me stay in bed;
It's just as well—well, fill the kettle....

I must have had that half dream again,
and though it wasn't fully her this time,
it must have been someone in the line
of blue eyes—(where the hell's the cream?)

She wasn't the first girl I had, I was a virgin lad.
That first one was to come later; I was raw.
That I wasn't her first boy was what I never saw.
My friends looked aside and said she just was "bad."

How could I know she'd come along?
How could I blame her for my pain?
But I hated her all the same;
not for the sin of it, but for the wrong.

Who's fault is this? I asked, and who's to blame?
How bad was what she'd done? (And was *he* the only one?)
Was it my pride that hurt? *Why* all his pain?

I was too young to bear it, but somehow one goes on.
It was hard to eat, I couldn't sleep, and how deep it cut
When my father said, "Forget her; she's only a slut."
I'm not sure how it ended; one day she just was gone.

Was the innocence mine or hers? I never could discover.
I saw her once, years later, looking careworn and harried.
She'd got fat, five kids, and no longer was married;
But if she was only a slut, how could I still love her?

Somehow I managed to love again; I continued to live,
but, how many that first frightening moment never seize,
"And from the dregs of life think to receive
what the first sprightly running could not give?"*

---

* John Dreyden, 1676.

Torment

Let me tell you of a love without glory—
a sighing, dying, lying, trying story—
where under swaying susurrating palms
he lay in her arms and breathed the balm
of the perfumed trades, of her sweet plumeria
mixed with the wild and delicate wisteria.
How, how could it be that in all this splendor
where nature's beauty cries out, Surrender!
How, in *those gentle trés riches belles heures,*
under those Aeolian *zephyrs sans rigueurs,*
how could that heart which strove so to love
not match the one that flutter'd like a dove?

How could those vipers of doubt and mistrust
in this paradise of sleepy softness thrust
their venomous heads into that brave breast,
invade a heart so pure that strove to invest
that enchanting creature whose mere desire
was surely, and purely, to set his loins afire!
But her love was of another kind, was blind
to his; *her* innocence was of a different mind.
She had discerned no trace in his face so dour
that he'd been taught thoughts of love too pure;
too late she saw she could not love just *anyone.*
But she adored him! the others were just in fun....

Othello Wasn't Jealous

Canto I

It was not jealousy that caused Othello to kill Desdemona,
　　　　But a torment; the anguish
that the living creature he believed to be exalted, divine,
　　　　heavenly, should be proven
sullied, used, unclean, impure, fallen; therefore, worthless.
　　　　He was disconsolate
in Desdemona's apparent lack of virtue, not jealous of her
　　　　faithlessness.
What broke his noble and aristocratic heart was that virtue
　　　　should so fall.
When he looked at her, so serene and happy, he could not
　　　　believe the detestable truth.
What he couldn't know, would not permit himself to accept,
　　　　was that she was happy
with him, in him, her deep love for him, the object he thought
　　　　she had betrayed.
But he had predeceased his adored object; he already was dead,
　　　　you see, spiritually.
But what if she *had* been faithless? Where, where is the
　　　　greater iniquity?
If she had been guilty and had shown him greater contrition,
　　　　could he have gone on?
Could *they* have gone on? If not jealousy or wounded pride
　　　　was it his inability to forgive,
if not forget? A genuine and spiritual experience not so much
　　　　of forgiveness,

which implies a transgression of some sort, but rather one of
    understanding, empathy,
and more important, acceptance? One thinks of Schoenberg's
    "A Transfigured Night,"
his musical adaptation of Dehmel's beautiful poem of the
    same name.

Canto II

Better this than continuing to wallow in self-pity, self-interest,
    and plain spite?
And what of her, this divine object he so valued, treasured,
    and exalted?
What if she *had* debased herself? The human soul, the spirit,
    is extraordinary;
It never soars so high as when the flesh had abased itself
    for a time in the gutter!
See a woman: beautiful, seemingly perfect, who has handled
    her share of excrement,
oh yes, literally as well as figuratively. Women can handle
    the coarser aspects of real life,
and the human condition generally, better than most men,
    who mainly are
infinitely more impractical, fanciful, than most women.

Canto III

Some men place women, conveniently docket them, into a
        a supra-natural state
that most women don't deserve, and which the more honest ones,
        would reject, if allowed to.
Women, placed in an ivory tower, or on a pedestal, but then there's
        Maugham and that back passage.*
Oh, however fair and smooth the skin, stench and corruption
        lie within; or, a tube
within a tube, usually about three-quarters full of excrement.
        Oh, woe to the fanciful.
Must they be Prospero's "stuff that dreams are made on" ?
        Why relegate women
to this status of semi-divinity that only serves to make them
        at best uncomfortable,
at worst impossible to be qualified for and uneasily perplexed
        as to why they
should be expected to maintain such other-worldly standards
        of propriety and virtue?
Why place young womanhood if not in an ivory tower then
        in a turret window
where she will wait, *virgo intacta,* yearning for her perfect and
        equally virtuous,
(if not equally celibate) consort to come, astride a white horse?

---

* This mixed comment from Somerset Maugham's *Cakes and Ale* is illustrative.
Writing some hundred years ago, Maugham is discussing women's plight in even
earlier literature when he says. "We know that women are habitually constipated,
but to represent them as being utterly devoid of a back passage seems to me an
excess of chivalry." Apparently, even the thought of sherbet was too excessive for
those earlier writers of whom Maugham spoke.

Canto IV

Later, oh, perhaps much later, a man may face the unhappy reality
        that women,
barring the fundamental physical differences, are little different
        than men, and then may
develop a tendency to seek compensation for this disillusionment
        by trying to bed
every available female he meets, as a sort of revenge for all that
        wasted time.
But that romantic impulse, though only a vestige of its former self,
        persists, and
though the misguided male knows, as he always did, no matter
        how deeply he tried
to bury such repulsive thoughts, that attractive females do not excrete
        orange sherbet
in little cellophane bags, he still insists that they be demur enough
        to permit him to
make advances, to initiate the action; in short, to be the aggressor
        in the sexual contest.

Canto V

Perhaps instead of continuing to assume a stance of
        wronged righteousness,
 like that of Patience on her pedestal, or that
        of a Christian
martyr smiling through the flames, or stoically counting
        the arrows with which
he has been shot as they pierce his body, or conversely
        (and much worse),

like a demon whose blackened heart is hell-bent on revenge—
      instead of any of that
fruitless though still very real agony, perhaps you'll see that
      life really is
too short to harbor any such disillusionment and bitterness;
      and to visit it on another human
whose life, despite what the actuaries say, is similarly short,
      you could instead
devote what little time you may have left, having accepted
      matters as they are,
to being if not happy at least content with your life. And it
      hardly needs saying
to those of you who have children, that your actions and your
      attitude will have
a serious and lasting impact on those children, whomever they
      may be living with.

Canto VI

Although in keeping with our new rules, today is the day
      of the antihero—
one thinks of the roles played by such actors as Dustin Hoffman,
      Richard Dreyfuss, Tom Hanks,
and so on; the mainly plain flawed men, who still manage to
      "get the girl"—
(does anyone look at Tom Hanks and see Cary Grant or
      Clark Gable? Why not?
The difference, my dear, is that those handsome older actors
      were adults!)
The fact is that the old fashioned hero still enjoys a good deal

of popularity;

I speak of such action figures as Rambo, Rocky, Indiana Jones,
       —and so on.

But this type of hero who is so very popular today causes one
       to wonder what

women seek in a man, other than the age-old sexual gratification,
       other than

a certain adrenal stimulation evoked by the man's fantastical
       physical exploits

(thanks in great part to Hollywood's special affects, stunt
       people, and now computer-

generated images, a whole new industry that is virtually becoming
       a new sub-culture).

Today's popular "heroes" are mainly shallow and uninteresting
       (when at rest).

Do today's women long for, if only in fantasy, the company
       of such men, or do they prefer

those who exhibit traits of deference, ineptitude self-effacement
       even cowardice

so strongly (men they can "mother") as to be almost as unrealistic
       as the fictional

and highly unlikely heroes of whom I just spoke? Trying to know
       what the "average" woman

wants in man is a little like trying to shoot pool with a hockey stick,
       trying to

evolve a precise rule that applies in every case is to risk your sanity.
       But still, I have

become convinced that women, who nonetheless generally are much
       more practical and

realistic than men, want the same qualities today that they always

have wanted in men:
strength (not necessarily physical), gentleness, intelligence, humor,
      understanding,
a degree of honesty, and the promise of some security in such
      mundane matters
as food, shelter, and assistance in the adequate rearing of children
      who may result
from a sexual union—all this, in most but not every case, being
      above or beyond
the sexual gratification I spoke of earlier that both should enjoy.

Canto VII

What most desirable women *don't* want—at least those I have known
      who were worth knowing
—are men who cannot pass a mirror without glancing at themselves,
      who talk about nothing
except themselves, their possessions (motor vehicles, clothing, real estate),
      in other words
those men who feel that because of their physical or material attributes
      women must
find them irresistible, and so are dumbfounded when they are rejected.
      Finally, though it may be
unjust that "older" men—assuming they are not grotesquely unattractive
      or wretchedly poor,
but who may be unassuming and interesting—can, if they wish to, enjoy
      the charms and favors of
"younger" women without taking too much trouble to do so,
      the converse is not true.

(Here one thinks of the late Helen Gurley Brown, trying so desperately
          "to stay in the game.")
Although this is nothing to gloat about, I must admit that the knowledge
          and experience of this
fact has brought me, however unjustly, some measure of comfort during
          these, my waning years
But I seem to have forgotten the disenchantment of the sad Othello
          in this long screed.
But then, to me, though pitiable enough, he seems eminently forgettable.

A Treasure

Billy Back of Beyond* got there first, but he wasn't
          qualified to speak
of such happy matters, whereas I, if you'll
          pardon the cheek,
have a vast experience in the domestic arts and
          sciences,
and in the course of that pursuit I have formed
          those alliances
which over many years and with many women
          in my *ménage*—
wives, mistresses, guests, and just women
          at large,
even comely domestics whom I have entertained
          in my garage—

---

* W.S. Maugham, whose friends called him "Bill" or "Billy," wrote "The Treasure" as
  well as "The Back of Beyond," which were in my opinion two of his best short stories.

have led me, over the years, to a greater or lesser
        degree,
to know what a tight-lipped (not always!) woman
        should be,
especially a servant-girl or woman, imbued with
        proper feudal spirit—
one who can welcome, give and take, joy, and not
        fear it,
who will cast her cap happily over the windmill
        with good cheer,
needful of no inducement to "have some Madeira,
        m'dear!"
And when her chores are done and she has baked our
        bread,
and peace descends on that sweet abode over which
        she spread
slight, light disorder which only heightens all
        her charms,
we shyly come together, and find our happiness in
        each others arms.

Now that I am old and replete with little ills;
        still, when,
despite all that, I have wealth—what joy to have
        her again!
Today, to go forth and bring home prey is too trying,
        too tedious a task—
Oh, would that I had *her* again! Aye, but alas, that is
        just too much to ask....

The Rambler

Did I love my mistress Gemma
more than I did my wife Emma?
Truly, this was a horny dilemma.

Once, on that holiday in Vienna,
I called my wife Emma—Gemma!
In London I called Gemma, Emma.

"This can't go on, that much is plain,"
I said one day to my old friend Jane.
She agreed, and so we left for Spain.

After a month of rain on the plain,
I discovered that Jane was just a pain,
so I left her and took the next plane.

I flew to Rome, so enchanting and handy,
where, though depressed, I felt very randy;
and there I met an American named Sandy.

Sandy made Emma and Gemma look plain;
while Jane, undoubtedly, still was a pain.
Unquestionably, their "loss" was my gain.

Now Sandy and I have established a nest,
somewhere, unnamed, away in the West,
far from former females and other pests.

But why, you may ask, would I take the time
to write something so remote from sublime?
The answer of course is, *it was easy to rhyme!*

The Merchants of Death

The Snowman

Standing in snow in the forest
As again it begins to snow,
I gaze from the edge of this forest
At the lights in that village below.

The skeletal frames in the hops fields
And the Calvary all covered with snow...
I ache for the warmth of that village,
For a peace I cannot hope to know.
From the dead silence around me
Comes a sadness—ineffable, deep;
What *is it* about this country
That can make a soldier weep?

The green-black firs behind me
Stand on and on in silence,
And evenly ranked in their thousands
Form a grand arboreal alliance.

These trees have stood here for centuries,
And though conscript and told where to grow,
They are linked to their brothers and sisters,
Would not march if told they must go.

These trees are indifferent to orders,
See no lines in the earth or the snow;
Ah, but trees know nothing of *borders,*
Unlike the men in that village below,

For a moment I'll stand here among them,
Knowing that soon I must go—
Perhaps before long I can join them,
Rooted, but free, in the snow.

*Il n' y a Pas Aucun Chemin de Fleuers**

They that had fought so well / Came through the jaws of Death,
Back from the mouth of Hell / All that was left of them....
When can their glory fade? / O the wild charge they made!
Honor the Light Brigade / Noble six hundred!

Il n' y a pas aucun chemin de fleuers qui conduit a la gloire.

Well, they were more like seven hundred (which didn't scan);
but in any case, thus Tennyson, and those glorious men of 1854.
When it was over that valley floor was littered with corpses,
thick with cannonballs, which lay no more than three feet apart.
It's hard to see glory in the senseless death of five hundred men,
harder still the useless killing of five hundred brave horses.

And then, when Crane's Boy sees those jaws of death opening
for *him,* he runs—cap and rifle gone, coat flying—with all the

* It isn't any path of flowers (that leads to glory).

horror of his imaginings on his face; only to return to that Hell,
not for glory, but for the sake of his friends who had remained.

And then, that bellicose pageant of science and industry, that
Great War, which made those splendid chargers obsolete and
changed the scarlet and pink and sky blue to khaki drill, and
which Scott Fitzgerald presciently called "The Last Love Battle."
Gone were those magnificent Lancers, Hussars, and Dragoons;
replaced by sandbags, duckboards, corrugated iron—and mud.
Paul Baümer sees men without mouths, jaws, or faces; while
the sun goes down, night comes, shells whine, life is at an end.

And then, when the reality no longer was supportable, endurable,
and certainly not explainable or justifiable, to Heller's absurd
theater, with Yossarian in the role of the wise buffoon, until the
inevitable horror of Snowden's guts welling out onto the floor....

And then the sheer clinical horror of the effects of a VC mine:
"They took off his testicles and penis, explored his abdomen,
took out his kidney and four inches of large bowel, sewed up his
liver... his left leg was removed by a left-hip disarticulation ..."*
And so on; on to electronic war, so glorified by those machines
children (young and old) and even off-duty soldiers love to play!

Yes, we have made great progress; but it seems that greedy Death,
though he still keeps pace, has slammed the door in Glory's face.
So then, where next? Does Glory but sleep behind that door? Then,
Leave it, I say! That bright tragic thing belongs to our ancestors.

---

* Ron Glasser, former Major, US Army Medical Corps, from his book *365 Days*.

But wait—

Is this an echo that I hear, from those who say they know not fear;
would-be soldiers who never see that songs of glory aren't sung,
that glory's just a *word,* when cannons blink and bump and growl,
and mortars thump and fragments howl, and sizzling steel finds
some tender, fear-heaving chest where a medal might have hung?

Listen! and you too shall hear them....

O the wild charge he made. He who would see Glory fade?
Dishonor the knave, dishonor *him* who that statement made!
O Good Just God, in Your wisdom *forbid* that ever Glory fade!

Missing in Action*

I'm still here where the sergeant left me.
So stop mooning about me; stop hoping
that I may be wandering about somewhere
with amnesia, or that I might be safe
if not happy in some prisoner of war camp.

I'm still *here*, where the sergeant left me.
It's just that they couldn't find a piece of me
that was big enough to identify as being *me*.
God knows what happened to my dog tags;

---

* The "voice from the grave" technique also has been used to good effect in such poems
as Thomas Hardy's "Ah, Are You Digging on My Grave?" and in John McCrae's "In
Flanders Field."

they couldn't even find those, either.

No, I'm still here where the sergeant left me,
where, as soon as he'd left, that shell came in.
But then, in another way I'm really *not* here,
and I'm damned glad that where I *really* am
I'm all together again (in a manner of speaking).

So do yourselves a favor: stop mooning, hoping
that I'm still having to go through what you do.
Yes, I'm still here where the sergeant left me;
that's all you have to know, except that I wish
I could tell you I'm not *there,* and I'm glad of it.

The O & E Department

Whenever money and circumstances permit it
we visit his grave "in a corner of a foreign field,"
where "the crosses row on row" go to the horizon.
We stand near his final resting place and hope
he may have found peace after all he had faced.
And we always cover him with fresh flowers....

We wanted something suitable, an inscription
to place there, where he rested, and chose this:
Sleep on, Beloved Son - Take Thy Gentle Rest.
As we two stand here, we share some solace,
knowing he has this little place we can visit.
When it's very still, I can almost hear his voice....

My God; hear my voice! When it was ended
I had not even a mouth with which to speak!
And oh! to think I'm here when I'm nowhere near,
but a hundred yards away, in that mass grave,
where they tumbled me in with a hundred others,
whole corpses and bits and pieces, odds and ends
of what once were my vital and cherished friends!

And their flowers! They cover me with flowers!
You cover nothing down there, barring worms
and perhaps a mole as it quietly makes its way
beneath this unsullied piece of earth far removed
from the great, grisly, stinking pit where I was laid.
Well, if you must condole as well do it over a mole,
and better never to visit that other great grisly hole.

So for God's sake, stay home, and think of me there,
while I thank God you could not hear my voice today.

Building Blocks

They weren't all I had, those alphabet blocks.
Later there was an Erector set, more intricate;
and then, when there was a little more money,
there even was an electric train set—
not an expensive one: the cars were made of tin,
and the engine wasn't much better;
it certainly wasn't one of those made to scale,
like the Lionel HO gauge beauties I'd seen

in a shop window a week before Christmas.
But still, my train was electric, and it ran
(sometimes too fast, and jumped off the track;
I can still smell that overheated transformer).

But then there were those ornate Richter blocks,*
made in Germany in the '30s (as the clouds gathered).
Made of sand and chalk, with a linseed oil varnish,
they were sold in a box painted with an exotic design:
an evocative female figure representing architecture.

They came in shapes such as Greek temple columns
that included Corinthian, Doric, and Ionic capitals.
Now that they have become popular with collectors,
I could sell them and retire again (if I'd kept them).
Ironic, but fitting somehow, that soon those Germans
were to lose so many real, ornate and stately buildings,
but still be left with their cherished Richter blocks.

The Messerschmidt

That day at the Museum of Science and Industry in New York.
An ME-109, just arrived from England, probably salvaged
from the many, along with those fallen Heinkels and Dorniers,
and Spitfires and Hurricanes, in the recent Battle of Britain.
It had no wings, just the fuselage and tail; still, quite a sight

---

* Invented by the Lilienthal brothers in the early 1930s, they have become popular
collectors' items, with a club in Germany that still distributes a monthly newsletter.

for me, a boy of twelve, who built model war planes.
I climbed up (I was permitted) and stuck my head into
that cramped cockpit (whose canopy was gone or just open).

I'd just come from the Metropolitan Museum of Art.
I had been taken there mainly to see the place itself,
but, happily, especially to see the armor and arms exhibit,
and I had wandered through the huge, high-ceilinged gallery,
gazing silently but in awe at those medieval suits of armor,
two-handed swords, battle axes, maces, and all the rest,
much of which was Germanic, from the Maximillian era.

Now, as I looked into that cockpit and tried to imagine
what that German pilot had looked like, my thoughts combined
with what I had seen earlier in that somber museum armory.
I thought of Von Richthofen, the Red Knight of Germany,
and of those other chivalric air warriors of the Great War.
(Born between the Wars, I knew more about the First one.)
And then I became aware of the odor that enveloped me.

Oh, that smell! That ineffable, piquant, sickeningly sweet,
stench which comes only from blood or human excrement.
My God, I didn't know it then, couldn't be sure, didn't want to be.
It must be the plane itself, I thought; if I'd known enough then
I might have said it was hydraulic fluid, spilled in the crash.
I wouldn't be sure for years, until I too went to another war.
Finally I had to admit it, much as I didn't want to, even then:
that poor young bastard of a pilot had soiled himself as he died!
much as a head-shot cock pheasant will, taken in mid-flight,
as now suddenly dead, he arcs towards to the unseen ground.

Old Goats and Kids
(*Dulce bellum inexpertis*)*

Those fourteen-year-old drummers and fifers
who were blown to bits at Albuhera
were boys, boy-soldiers. Those who lived
to be a few years older became men.
None of them ever were called "kids";
lads or boys perhaps, but never "kids."
If you're a soldier you're no longer a "kid";
you're entitled to be called a man.
It is those Old Goats, safe at home—
most of whom never smelled the smoke,
heard the thunder of those distant guns,
quailed under the burst of their shells—
who persist in calling them boys, or kids.

One July (near Albert)

From the east he came that summer's day, and
glowering, made his crablike way, and the beast
who'd blinked and bumped and growled all night
now merely coughed and sulked in seeming spite.

---

* War is delightful to the inexperienced—inscribed on the tomb of Henry III at
Westminster Abby.

Mere mortals crouched on feet of clay, wiped dew
from steel, and mutely begged to live another day;
saw beauty in corrupted earth or shattered tree.
Faintly blessed, they knew not about the "Z."*

Against pink clouds and welkin blue
The Golden Lady held her Babe to view—†
But soon such kindlier shades were swept away,
and then more human hues began to dress the clay.

O God! O God! what could the Lady say?
Blood-red, bone-white, black flesh, yellow clay,
all day all day, till finally Phoebus rolled away.
Unblinking, unthinking, so late, too late—
Unseeing, uncaring, on that perfect summer's day,
One July, near Albert, that perfect summer's day.

Peace at Warlencourt

They looked from a distance like
hundreds of contented sheep lying
on a hillside, and drawing nearer
one saw they *were* sheep—men-sheep;

---

* At the Battle of the Somme on 1 July 1916 the German defense included eight Maxim machine guns which delivered a withering, grazing, enfilade fire on the advancing British lines, which sustained 60,000 casualties, with 20,000 dead on that first day. The "battle" would last another four months.

† The "Lady" was a statue of the Golden Virgin and Child atop the Basilica of the church in Albert, which earlier, having been hit by artillery fire, now was leaning precariously below the horizontal, and seemingly throwing her child into the battle.

some still clad in remnants of *feld grau*
(*grauen* might be a more suitable word),
some in their tattered rags of khaki drill;
but they lay in such profuse confusion
that some—what was left of them—seemed
to be wearing one another's uniforms!

Here, a belt buckle, toed out of the mud, says
Gott Mit Uns (like the one Hemingway wore).
On a hilltop a large, weathered stone cross
proclaimed simply but eloquently the single word:
Friede. I know how Hemingway found peace,
and as I turn this filthy battered belt buckle over
I wonder who *its* owner was; and I wonder also
who indeed God *had* been with in this desert, in
this wasted but peaceful desert called Warlencourt.

How Can You?

How can you say "we" have won when
all we have won is the right to be buried
at Arlington or, if the place is too full of
civilian presidents or other pretenders,
at some other bone yard of the brave?

It all has been said. How can I, whose voice
cannot even be heard, improve or add to
those gut-wrenching, eloquent appeals of
Sassoon, Rosenberg, Larkin, or Blunden? If
they could not make you see it, how can I?

But do you *really* want to know the Hell
where youth and laughter go? When you wake
do you feel a rat has leaped *your* hand? Will you
ever let us know innocence again? Can *you* not see
a harmless young shepherd in a soldier's coat?

Death Be Not Proud

The Man in the Moon

I'm going to see the man in the moon,
soon, I hope (and fear), soon.
He said he would wait for me; not to hurry;
he told me to look for him in the crescent,
when that bottom-heavy cantaloupe slice
makes a couch on which he can lie,
with his old battered cloth cap cocked forward
over his eyes, and his feet crossed, and with
his big battered hands clasped behind his head.

I went out tonight, a few minutes ago,
and across the fields of snow, saw *his* moon,
hanging low, his cantaloupe portion arced low,
just above the silver snow horizon,
glowing warmly yellow in the dark, frozen sky,
and for a moment thought I saw him (could it be?);
and then, for just an instant, a fleeting moment,
I thought I saw a lazy arm raised, a brief wave,
a half-salute, in my direction, or was it just a wisp
of winter cloud, passing over that butter-sickle moon?

A Wastrel's Prayer

O, Lord, this very night could be the one in which
I pay my final dues, check out,
cash in my chips, turn in my dinner pail;
It all comes to the same thing.
So now let me turn to St. Luke (12:20 in your Books),
and pay attention when he talks to me
about all that dross I've so assiduously gathered in.
For perhaps *this very night shall my soul*
be required of me; and, if so, then whose shall those
things be which I've so selfishly provided; yes, provided,
but solely for myself? So *let* my body *rot*, dear Lord,
and let crumble all that useless dross as well;
but please, O God! let my mind, my soul, go on;
let it go on, "to strive, to seek, to find, and not to yield"
to those base, ruinous cravings of my egoism.

The Netherlands

We'll all meet in the Netherlands; well, maybe
you won't all be together, but wherever *you* are
somehow you'll all know where the others are.
In the Netherlands you'll all be seen equally; you
won't be taller or stronger, or better looking,
or more talented than anyone else. She won't
be able to cheat on you, or you on her, and your
boss (even if he's where *you* are) won't be able
to tell you how far you fall short of the mark.

So we'll meet in the Netherlands; yes, in fact,
I'll take you there, and we won't go Dutch, it'll
all be on me, just to be certain you get there.
For am I not truly God's man? Then for *God's* sake,
be ready when I come to take you to the Netherlands!

Never Such Innocence Again

Barnegat Bay
(A Prose Poem)

The stone made five short-lived pools on
that flat black surface and sank with the sixth
as I stood one foggy day in the cove of the Bay,
and through the mists of time I recalled
those flotsam and jetsam bits of memories;
some, the newer ones, bobbed on the surface
while others, weeded with age, had to be dredged
up from the depths to which they had sunk….

How long *did* my eighth-grade friend cling
to that overturned skiff (while his older
brother swam for help, and lived) before he
slipped beneath those brackish, blackish waves
that day The Bay was wild and unforgiving?
We only won the game that week because
he wasn't there to captain the other team.

The drowning near the pier was real. I saw it.
I didn't have to imagine it, like trying to see
Jimmy trying to hang on to the overturned boat.
Besides, the one by the pier was a grown up man.
I was sitting on a piling, eating an apple, watching
as a man tied up his sailboat to an anchor buoy
and, still wearing his white low-cut sneakers,

lowered himself into the chest-high water and
started walking, pushing two oars in front of him.
All of a sudden there were just those two oars,
bobbing about on the surface—he was gone!
Bert, the gravelly-voiced expatriate Englishman
who had been gassed in the Great War (they said)
and now rented flat-bottomed rowboats, went out,
and grappling with an anchor, finally hooked a leg,
and the first thing I saw was a muddy white sneaker.
They said he'd stepped into a hole where, I guess,
his other sneaker still was (and maybe still is).

I remember the stove-in skiff I found in late May
and tried to fix, that summer when school was out,
as often as I could get down there, to The Cove,
long into June. My father came along one day, and
shook his head. "I don't know…" he said, but still
he gave me scraps of wood, pounds of putty, nails,
and his old hammer and saw, and time to go and work.
But it was no good. I never could get it right, to float.
At least Jimmy had had a floating boat to cling to
before he had to let go. But then if he'd had *my* boat
maybe he couldn't have gotten so far from shore….

"N' Street was two hundred yards of bulkheads,
boat slips, and berthings, where that old, red-faced,
white-bearded Mr. Rheibold—he seemed old to me,
with his full white beard and hair; a veritable Santa
who my older brother called Mr. Dry Bones—built
boats, big inboard-engine power boats, by hand, alone,

right down to the last brass screw. Old Dry Bones and my father built eel traps, in those days before dredging sucked all the eels out of that mystical Eel Pit the old-timers always talked about. And then old Mr. Gabriel (I was very young then, in those misty old times), the tinsmith and hunter of ten-gauge shotgun fame, would smoke the eels, and anything else we might bring him.

I'd look forward to when they emptied the traps, and at last one day they let me do it, the way I'd watched eagerly my father and Dry Bones do it many times. Hands in the Bay water, hands in the sand, then grab those black devils (some bigger around than my arm) fore and aft, then quick into the gunny sack with 'em! Once, one hooked its teeth into Rheibold's shoulder, and its writhing near three feet of muscle tore a strip of skin to his elbow. The old boy winced with pain, plucked it off his arm, and said, "You, son of a bitch, I'll eat you first!" Then he went for the first aid kit. But it was even worse when a sack full of eels got out of our kitchen sink during the night. When my mother went in to make the coffee the next morning nobody in the whole house needed an alarm clock.

I remember seaweed of all kinds, but mainly the great racks of stringy, smelly, dark-green stuff which would turn brownish-blackish when beached by the tides and which we used, wet, as a bed for the crabs—the softies, paper backs, the tin backs. And those venerable, in fact Devonian, horseshoe crabs,

unchanged in almost 400,000 years, which we
didn't eat but that too often were gigged by boys
with hunting knives lashed to broom handles. And
minnows, thousands of them, and the evil looking
blowfish, with their little gap teeth that snagged the
hook, to be punted back once they'd puffed up
(but delicious if you had patience and a sharp knife).
And, oh yes, barnacles! about which I learned all I
needed to know when I tried climbing out of the Bay
on a pier piling the day I had taught myself to swim.
(I threw my favorite ball out beyond the shallows
and there was no one else to go and get it for me.)

The wrecked houseboat my friends took me to see
one day, where illicit rendezvous were said to be held,
and nearby, on the ground, the evidence in the form
of several strange and yellowed rubber rings which,
I was told, were used somehow in these love trysts.
The War. Sailors on liberty with their rubber rings…
blimps from Lakehurst, dwarfed by the memory of
the majestic Hindenburg which, several years earlier,
first flew south, only a thousand feet over our house,
before its terrible rendezvous with who knows what?
We went next day in the old Ford to see its skeleton.
Ice skating over the ice humps, ice hockey, crack the
whip, sail skating with an old bed sheet and disaster
at the little pier when I couldn't stop or turn in time.

Pelican Island, which joined the quarter-mile and mile
and a quarter wooden bridges, both set afire by careless
tourist cigarettes several times each season. We got our
revenge in knowing how those tourists would sweat,
and curse, and *wait* when the big bridge draw would
go up for one of *our* tall-masted sailboats to go by.
Little Pelican Island really had pelicans once,
though that was long before my time, I was told.
And then later, driving the old heap at high speed
over the lightless big bridge and turning off the
headlights to frighten (impress?) that night's date.
College and coming home in summer to sail the
"G" sloop, and the almost too-long swim in to get
the dingy for a tow on a flat, too-calm, hot day.
Drinks, pretty girls, chatter, and a good lunch on
Barnegat Inlet sole afterward. Dancing at the Club.

But now is now. The eels have been dredged, the
horseshoe crabs all gigged out of existence, the
blue crabs overfished by greedy New York
fishmongers, the minnows seined by the
eaters of small fish down from Newark,
the wooden bridges replaced by ugly
fireproof concrete and uglier steel.
The Bay doesn't seem to freeze
solid the way it once did, and
those pelicans all a long-
gone memory,
All gone...

But since I no longer live here—I went away long,
long ago—I ask myself, Does this really matter?
I see no more flat stones to skip across the water;
I must have used all of them up. Anyway, it's time
I went, anyhow.

Little Red Wooden Fish

On the boardwalk—the Midway, we used to call it—
when my most prized toy was a submarine: a U-boat,
as they came to be known a few years later; the ones
that started sinking all those tankers that came out of
the Esso tank farms around Perth Amboy, the ones
we could see burning on the horizon late at night.
I used to play with that sub in the tub by the hour.
Back then, I learned to love water, and everything in it.

Anyway, on that boardwalk, that Midway, my favorite
stop, barring the Tompkins iced cream stand, was this
little place that had a sort of galvanized iron trough,
placed low enough so that I could stand and look down
into it and see the water flowing through it. And as I
stood and watched I could see little wooden fish go by.
Once painted a bright red they now were faded, chipped,
and dull. They had brass rings in their noses (well, where
their noses would be, I guess, if fish had noses),
and on their sides they had little round brass plates
nailed on them, each with a different number stamped
on it, from one to ten, I think. And now that I do think
about it, that was what kept those fish half submerged.

Well, the man behind the trough that separated him
from us, like the counters at the other stands, like the
wheel of fortune stands, this man had several little
fishing poles that he walked up and down with that had
short strings attached to them, and hooks, brass hooks,
on the ends of the strings, and if whoever had taken me
to that place gave the man a dime, he would give me
a pole and I could go fishing in the water going past!

You couldn't miss. I always caught a fish, no matter
how long it might take me. The fish just kept coming by
in endless procession and profusion (at the time I didn't
know they were the same battered old fish going around
and around through that tank somehow, like the soldiers
marching by in a low budget stage show circling behind
the sets, giving us a sense of Caesar's limitless legions).
And I would fish, and fish, until with joy unbounded,
I hooked one. Then the man would take the little red fish
off the hook, reach up to one of the shelves behind him,
and give me a small, cheap prize—a monkey on a string,
or a pinwheel. He never smiled when he gave me my prize.

And later, years later, I heard about shooting fish in a barrel.
And many years after that, in Vietnam, I saw how it is done.

Carousel

You can pay and get on with everyone else, more or less under
    supervision; and, when the bell rings, off you go!
Or, if you are young and agile, and maybe a bit of a
    rule-breaker, and not too scared, or
you just haven't got the price of a ticket, you can jump on
    when it's already in motion.

You'd better be ready to jump off though, when the man comes
    to collect the tickets.
You might stumble or even fall when you try to jump on or off;
    but with more experience,
you might become proficient at this beating of the cost,
    at least to the extent of carousels.

Oh! all the animals! Lions, and tigers (but no bears or bulls),
    and wild-eyed horses and tame horses;
and some go up and down and others stay stately still,
    where they'd been placed and had always been.
But even the ones that move only go up and down, so
    there is no linear progress; and even if there were,
the overall path is circular, so you always end up
    right where you started.

The lions and tigers on the outer edge don't have ups and downs,
    so they are handy to stand next to
and hold on to so you can reach out and try for the brass ring
    (or gold, if you see it that way) among all that steel.
There even are regular seats: big swans, or little carriages

or sleighs, for the very young, or the very old.
And oh, the music! that wonderful heavy-tinny Wurlitzer
    band-organ that ends when the carousel stops.

But even if you don't get the brass ring, and the ticket man
    (who somehow saw you jump on)
doesn't catch you before you jump off, there is always
    the frozen custard stand nearby, if you have a dime;
or later, when you were older and could appreciate food, that
    cheap little Italian place, not a block away.
It wasn't Italy (yet), but it could be, if you dreamed a little,
    just a little....

A carousel is a kind of rotating earlier-day Disneyland,
    with lots of ups and downs,
but all self-contained, and much cheaper too (if you pay at all).
    But if you like to ride the carousel
you are apt to feel—especially if you have to pay for it—
    when that last bell rings,
that the ride was too short; especially if you only had the
    price of one ticket,
didn't get the brass ring, and you couldn't, or wouldn't,
    jump on or off.

Jeux D' Enfants

Je Ne Regrette Rien?

No regrets? Nonsense.
The interview; the question; and then the answer:
No, I haven't any regrets;
if I had to do it again I wouldn't change anything.
That person either is mentally deranged,
a blatant liar, or just a conscienceless, arrogant egoist;
(and the interviewer probably a sycophantic fool).

I, on the other hand, have a list which would
make all your New Year's resolutions,
all of them, even if you've lived a very long time,
look insignificant by comparison.
Oh, if I had it to do again! If I were given the chance,
to live it again, what I would try to do!
And, oh! perhaps what is more important,
what would I try hard, very hard, not to do?

The Little Sparrow was just singing us a song.

Grades of Clay

Crichton, Updike, interviewed on television:
"To what do you ascribe your great success?"
Blah, blah, (replete with cant, false modesty),
"I saw this, thought about this, heard this," etc.
often ending with: "I guess I've been very lucky."
Lucky? *Lucky?* Yes, but avoid the main reason.

Not a word about the people who buy the books—
who don't know *scata* from a good grade of clay.
Just once, oh, just *once!* how I'd like to hear:
"I'm pandering to a bunch of illiterate morons.
It's too easy. I just give 'em what they lap up."

It's like the fast food industry here in America:
chocolate pizza? (God!); peanut butter chicken?
As in fishing, "coarse feeders" bite at anything.
But neither the interviewer nor that "celebrity"
ever addresses that prime reason for "success,"
in any of the so-called "arts" in today's society.

And this is to say nothing about other activities:
scholarship, conversation, philosophical thought,
dining (!), personal appearance, transportation—
in a word, the popular American culture *per se*,
in which the Great Unwashed of today recreate
(and unfortunately they continue to procreate).

Alas, you can't make a good pot from poor clay.

Cotton Candy
(A Prose Poem)

No Schiller, Goethe, Tolstoy, Shakespeare, Manzoni.
No national philosophy, or coherent cultural values.
Two meanings has Culture: what we are and what we
should-could be (*Vorrei vogliare quello che non voglio*).*
What we have is great emphasis on the physical life.
We make a virtue out of our isolationism, coarseness,
philistinism; with no solid art, no linguistic ability.
Could Lady Radnor ever compete with Lady Gaga?[†]
Can we boast a politician like Paderewski or Schmidt?
No, but we had a pianist like Harry Truman, and latterly
an amateur President-saxophone player. We must face it:
we're a nation (we can't be a race) of disparate peasants,
religious morons, and criminals, from the highest halls
of power to the lowest ghetto. We have no central stem;
we're a bush, not a tree, and, alas, a bush that produces
bitter fruit and no pretty flowers. Democracy has proven
to be its own worst enemy (cf. Alexis De Tocqueville).

The Great Leveling Process always works downward;
we don't reach for the stars, except those in Hollywood
and in our clumsy space programs. We're happy to grovel
in the mud, where we feel less challenged, more secure.

---

* I would want to want that which I don't want—an old Florentine adage.
† The British composer, Countess Lady Radnor, wrote and conducted her "Lady Radnor's Suite" at its first performance in 1894.

If anyone objects we flex our muscles, actual or military.
Our answer to everything is brutish, bullying, physical;
yes, we're only cotton candy: cheap, sweet, no substance.

Cell Phones

Up link, down link, and so forth; all very well;
but you never know where the person *is,*
the one you're talking to. "Where're you calling from?"
"Me? I'm parked in your driveway" (with a gun?).

As in "perks" (perquisites, which few people can spell)
few people know that "cell," much as "phone" obtains
from telephone, derives from cellular
(and even I don't know what that means, anent phones).

Well, in a manner of speaking we're all in cells;
we're all confined by our own technology, whether
on the receiving or sending end of things.
And if the trend persists, technology, once our slave,
well may, even before we're eradicated by global heat,
become the master, unless *Someone* turns off the lights.

What Cheek!

What is your email address?
What is an email address?

You could send us an email.
Once again, what is an email?

Text me when you get there.
Send you a *book*? *What* book?

Well, we can protect you against
identity theft on the internet....

I can save you the trouble there—
I'm not *on* that bloody internet.

Toys R Us

Seventeen-million toys recalled because of lead *traces*,
while 7/8ths of all children have not one toy, perhaps not
even enough food, and meanwhile the world is in flames;
and we're shooting each other to death by the thousands,
or we're dying by our own hand of a drug overdose, or
dying from obesity, and we're probably the only nation
whose adults avidly watch *cartoons* on prime-time TV,
when we're not roaring around in go-carts, or on ATVs,
or on snowmobiles, dirt-bikes, or other raucous vehicles.
Meanwhile, our soldiers are so cluttered with gadgets

have so many "add-ons," as to be almost incompetent.

Each winter my mother would make a bean bag or two—
using an empty two-pound salt sack full of white beans—
with which my little sister and I played, in the house.
(Those beans were washed, cooked, and eaten in spring.)
Sometimes we were allowed to set up a little shop,
using canned or boxed food and homemade paper money,
while alternating the roles of shopkeeper and patron.

In the warmer weather, when storm drains overflowed,
and the clean rainwater flowed freely along the curbs,
a wooden cheese box with a popsicle stick for a mast
and an old handkerchief for a sail gave me that little boat
I liked to watch as the current made the sail meaningless.
On rainy days I played with my little, sturdy toy soldiers,
brave, colorful, and all of which were cast from solid lead.

One day I found a nickel, on the street I stood so close to,
gave it to my Mother, and got a comic book for my honesty;
because *then*, for a nickel you could buy that popsicle,
or a Coke, or any candy bar, a hot dog, or a mug of root beer,
or make a phone call, or even ride the subway for two hours.

As I grew older, I fought duels with my friends, in my yard,
using lath-stick-swords, dented ashcan lids as bucklers,
and an even more battered old aluminum pot for a helmet.
Later on, I was hitting small stones with a heavier stick,
and acquiring a batting eye which even later would make me
first choice when we chose up sides for sandlot baseball.

Even still, until I got to high school and saw new equipment,
I'd played with black baseballs (taped) and split bats (taped), and
I ran races in street shoes; later, with track spikes, I could fly!
Today, kids who aren't too fat, with $1000 worth of equipment,
most of them, couldn't hit a bull in the ass with a bass fiddle,
even if somehow they were standing on the poor bull's back.

Perhaps, instead of recalling all those silly, costly lead toys,
we should outlaw all that lead we use in useless wars,
or food which is killing our fat kids routinely in our schools.
As for me, despite all that asbestos I tore out of old buildings
and all those lead ingots I melted to caulk cast-iron stacks;
and later, after twenty years of parachute infantry service,
all those filterless Camels I've smoked for seventy years,
here am I, four-score and eight years later, lighting one up,
while I take a brief break from splitting my own firewood,
and recalling those beanbags my loving mother sewed.

Bonnie Beasties

The Feudal Spirit
(A Conversation with the Duchess of Dutch Hill)

Yes, Your Grace, he does derive from simple stock—
in trade, I think they were, or perhaps gentle farmers.
But he does have at least one redeeming quality—
Just look at his coat, My Lady! —is it not Princely?
Oh yes, it must be worth at least fifty guineas, I agree.
But born on the wrong side of the blanket, you say?
Umm, yes, perchance he was. A passing gentleman,
it may have been, perhaps even one of noble birth,
who dallied, briefly, but did not tarry, and who was
the giver of that coat? I think we shall never know;
his family is typically reticent about such matters.
I see him as a Dickensian waif, if you will, My Lady,
of no social standing, but with a good quality inside.
Yes, Your Grace, I will take him in hand, and I shall
do my best, Ma'am, to raise him to your expectations.
And there is every hope that, with proper nurturing
and what with your aristocratic influence, someday
he may, just may someday appear on the Honors List!

The Prince of Darkness

If he were in the navy he'd be a cruiser or a destroyer
        or perhaps even a submarine—
sometimes even a trawler, as he drags God-knows-what-
        next along behind him.
In the world of cats he's a superman, nay, a super *cat,*
        able to leap if not tall buildings
then tall objects, pieces of furniture, at a single bound.
        I'd hate to see him try to stop a bullet,
although I know he'd try (there have been times I've
        wanted to shoot him myself). And
if he can't pass a speeding train, he's faster than I am,
        and proves it when he races past me,
down the hall or stairs. He's clean as a coon, strong as
        an ox, stubborn as a mule, agile as
an ape, smart as a fox, and courageous as a lion; a dark
        storm cloud with a silver lining,
a silver streak. In the exuberance of youth he bounds
        through (or over) tall grass
with the quick grace of an impala or a gazelle.
        He's the Mad, the Blue, the *stamme*r Max—
who, even in his quiet moments, as he lies at my feet
        looking thoughtful, seemingly sonorously
saying his prayers, doubtless is thinking about and planning
        his next escapade. He's Max; and he's
Pascal's, not Peck's bad boy; and every day, that's right,
        every day, I decide to give him away—

until I pick him up, and he stares steadily and earnestly
into my eyes as he places his velvet paws
gently, gently against my mouth, pressing my lips, gently,
as if to stop what I just am about to say....

Swallows

They came, in the early spring; they built, they
nested,
and they produced many offspring, and they
nurtured them;
and during the course of all this they fouled my
back porch
with their droppings and with dead baby birds,
dropping;
to the extent that I stopped taking my lunch there.
So in the fall
I cleaned up the mess, removed two tiny and sere
ant-ridden bodies,
overlooked during the summer, and closed up that
two-inch space
in the corner, and dismissed my unsavory aviary
summer.

When the nesting birds came back next spring they
were flurried, frantic;
and after several desperate attempts to force the
barricade

an expectant mother loudly scolded the world
      generally,
then left, still complaining, and I went on with
      my lunch.
"I won't worship these beastly transient temporal
      'treasures!'—
And all this pap about spotted owls and kangaroo
      rats!" I told
myself staunchly. "It's hard enough to retain and
      enjoy what
little Man has without having to accommodate a
      family
of raucous, lice-ridden, filthy birds" I muttered as
      I brought out
the main course, and tranquilly sipped a little wine
      in blessed silence....

Then somehow, I found myself listening for that thin
      piping and chirping,
and for the rushing and fluttering of hurried wings as a
      peripatetic mother
arrived with her small offerings, gleaned from the
      newly-mown lawn.
And the little game hen I had just tasted turned to
      ashes in my mouth....
No matter how hard I tried to put this nonsense aside,
      no matter
how I rationalized all this with Man's reason, I just
      could not swallow.[*]

---

[*] Something about a wise bird not fouling its own nest?

Sea Horses

As a boy I'd look forward to going round
with my father for our weekly fish, early
on Friday mornings to the local net pound*
to provide for Friday's mandatory dish.

We had to leave early so as to arrive
when those lap-strake boats came in,
with myriad types of fish, some still alive,
flopping in their baskets or waggling a fin.

But fish were just fish—what did I care?
(unless a Mako or a Blue Fin got trapped in a net).
I went mostly to see the horses, chained in pairs
to the fish-filled boats; huge horses, lathered in sweat.

Their great dappled necks all corded with strain
as with massive heads bent, heads big as me,
they toiled up the beach in sun or in rain,
pulled the boats on the rollers, up from the sea.

The tall Nordic masters of these equine giants
used no whips or jibes, or curses or threats;
they seemed to elicit easy compliance
just with words spoken softly, as if to pets....

---

* Scandinavian immigrants had established a pound net industry on South New Jersey shore.

Then, as sometimes happens when one comes of age,
I had to leave my old village and go far afield....
And when the war finally ended (and peace again raged)
They let me go home till my wounds had healed.

My mother was gone, but my father was there,
and we went to the pub where we each bought a round.
To mask our unease as he tried not to stare
I asked if on Fridays he still went to the pound.

"Sometimes," he said as he looked his beer.
"But since fish for Friday's no longer a factor,
and your mother, of course, no longer is here...
heard that those horses were replaced by tractors?"

I thought of those horses, with hooves big as pie tins,
whose live, labored breathing was replaced by the clank
of the treads of the tractors with their rackety din—
and I heard three men screaming, trapped in a burning tank.

En Fin La Paix

Grief Relief

The blow falls like the headsman's axe,
and for who knows how many moments
(or years) your eyes are still sightful,
your brain functions, *elan vital* remains.

With shaking hands you light a cigarette,
or aimlessly straighten a picture,
or notice your shoelace is untied and stoop
to re-tie it, and so go on with your life....
Your life; or perhaps now, just half a life.

End or Beginning?

An end, or a beginning—
or does the end merely end the beginning?
And is there then another Beginning?
When we go home, and the slow walking ends,
and the sad talking begins, where does *it* go,
what does it say, if there is an It?

After El Alamein Churchill said:
"Now this is not the end.
It is not even the beginning of the end.

But it is, perhaps, the end of the beginning."
The beginning of what? To him—Victory.
But do *we* vanquish Death by dying?

If the end merely is that, falling into naught,
I can stop here; but if it does signal Donne's
"... one short sleep past, we wake eternally"
I can spend an eternity trying to know why;
like a comedian, perhaps, just killing time;
or, like a tragedian, merely killing eternity.*

Sintram's Cavalier†

I knew him though we've never met, He came by often
in former times, when I was younger.
Sometimes he would go past a window; I could see him.
Sometimes I wouldn't see him, but I could hear him.
Sometimes I couldn't see him or hear him,
But I knew he was there, just outside a door.
A few times I wished he'd just came in, present
himself, and have it done. But he never did.

Now he's not so close (or so it seems) and yet,
he's closer. He's not so far away that I don't know
he's there. And somehow, though I don't really see him,
as I so often did, I know he's moving, biding his time,

---

* See Miguel De Unamuno's *Prologue to San Manuel Bueno.*
† See Albrecht Dürer's (1471-1528) *The Knight, Death, and Satan.*

a little closer every day, looking at my doors and windows;
not looking *in* my widows, but seeing them, seeing
which way he can go in, when he is close enough.
I won't go out to meet him; he'll have to come inside.

A Celestial Library

Heaven? Paradise? What are they, or where?
Let us stay with "what," never mind where;
you'll never be able to understand that
until you get there—if it's there.
But *what* is it, for anyone, especially for you.
More to the point, what do you *want* it to be?

Some say it's an eternal state of happiness;
a reward for having lived a good and moral life.
Well, if that's true it'll be under-populated.
Some may ask, "How good, how holy are you?"
How could one be as happy as the next person
if one wasn't as good or holy as *that* person?

Try this. You won't *know,* and *he* won't know.
(All right, so as not to offend the ladies, "she,"
to satisfy those tense divinities of feminism.)
So each will know the happiness he deserves,
and will never know someone else is happier!
And, as I see it, you can't say fairer than that.

I have not been as good or as moral as I could,
so I can't and don't expect to get what I could
had my life been as good or holy as it should,
but if what's in that previous stanza is certain,
then when it's my turn to take the final curtain
I'll hope my sanctuary will be Shakespearean.

I'll hope my destination is a celestial library,
with an endless supply of superb literature,
with books never read, burned at Alexandria,
books never written by my favorite authors,
a librarian who speaks to me in six languages,
and of course no fee charged for overdue books.

Printed in the United States
by Baker & Taylor Publisher Services